GW00503825

Chelsea

Edited by
CLIVE BATTY

CARLTON
BOOKS

This edition published in 2007
First published by Carlton Books 2003
Reprinted with updates in 2006

This book is not an officially licensed product of
Chelsea Football Club

A CIP catalogue record for this book is available
from the British Library.

ISBN 978 1 84442 167 1

Printed in Singapore

INTRODUCTION

Forget 'The Mousetrap', the longest-running, most dramatic show the West End has to offer is staged at Stamford Bridge, SW6. Curtain up 3pm, every other Saturday – unless, of course, the TV companies rule otherwise. Reviews have been mixed over the years, but for jaw-dropping plot twists the multi-million-pound production that is 'The Blues' simply can't be topped. Ecstatic highs, depth-plumbing lows, silverware and scandal, with an all-star cast list drawn from the four corners of the globe, this show has the lot.

No wonder, then, that so many people have so much to say about Chelsea, London's undisputed glamour club. In this small but perfectly formed (think 'Shaun Wright-Phillips') collection of quotes, performers past and present, famous fans and an even more famous manager reveal why, for them, Blue really is the colour.

'Life is never dull at Stamford Bridge.'

Ken Bates

❝I've played for some big clubs but Chelsea were the tops. I loved the place, still do.**❞**

Mickey Thomas

‘Becoming a Chelsea director was one of the most marvellous things that has happened in my life.’

Lord Attenborough

> **❛**I used to be a keen supporter of Chelsea. Peter Osgood was my favourite player and I chose the number nine shirt for school matches because it was the one he wore.**❜**

Frank Bruno, *August 1986*

'Many a time I've rushed back to London to watch a game. I've played exhibition matches in Newcastle, for example, and then left at nine o'clock the next morning to get to Chelsea in time.**'**

Jimmy White, *April 1986*

❝Chelsea were the natural team for me to support. I would catch the 45 bus from Loughborough Junction to Battersea Bridge, and then walk across the bridge. I'd supported them earlier, but I actually started going in the year they won the Championship, 1954–55.❞

John Major, *August 1990*

❝I was so happy to hear those Chelsea cheers. I could have wept. That wonderful crowd. They had been taking it on the chin for 50 years and always come up smiling. How well they deserved to have something to cheer about now.**❞**

Captain **Roy Bentley** *after Chelsea's only Championship win, April 1955*

❝I would love to relive those days at Chelsea – they were wonderful times.**❞**

Jimmy Greaves, *August 1985*

❛Chelsea has always been my first love. I'd have liked to have spent the whole of my career at Stamford Bridge, but it was not to be. I always have a special place in my football heart for Chelsea.**❜**

Terry Venables, *January 1991*

"I didn't get that worked-up in the dressing room. Instead, I used to read the programme to see who I had to kick that week."

Ron 'Chopper' Harris

❝I played against Ron Harris and he frightened the life out of me. Thankfully, he never whacked me, and I appreciate that.**❞**

Hull City manager **Peter Taylor**

❝Peter Bonetti turned to me and said, "Who's that tasty-looking blonde in the corner?" I told him that it was my wife Daphne, and thought to myself that even the great Chelsea players have human instincts like the rest of us.❞

'Likely Lads' actor **Rodney Bewes**,
November 1985

❝I remember working in Rome for eight months on a film called 'Cleopatra', starring Elizabeth Taylor and Richard Burton. I used to fly to London every Friday, watch Chelsea on the Saturday, play charity football on the Sunday and then fly back!❞

'Man About the House' actor **Richard O'Sullivan**, September 1985

'Tommy Docherty and Ron 'Chopper' Harris invented soccer violence. It's when they retired that it spread to the terraces. '

Peter Osgood

❝Peter Osgood has never been replaced since the day Chelsea sold him.**❞**

Alan Hudson, *January 2001*

❝Skilful as he was, Ossie could dish it out and I was no shrinking violet. We hated each other with venom.❞

Frank McLintock, *captain of Arsenal's 1971 Double-winning team*

❝I like to think that, apart from being a bit of a butcher, I've something else to offer.**❞**

Ron Harris, *1979*

What they say about footballers being ignorant is rubbish. I spoke to a couple yesterday and they were quite intelligent.

Raquel Welch, *after a visit to the Bridge in 1973*

❝I'm a goalkeeper, so I expected the outfield players to gang up on me at some point.**❞**

Peter Bonetti, *after being voted off a 'footballers' special' edition of 'The Weakest Link'*

'I said I wanted the same car as James Bond and the reporter got the wrong end of the stick and said I wanted to be James Bond!'

Joe Cole, *August 2003*

❝ I'd like to be Sean Connery, 007 agent. **❞**

Gianluca Vialli, *February 1998*

‎**❛**Hoddle was one of my idols and it would have been brilliant to link up with the likes of Ruud Gullit, Dennis Wise and Mark Hughes.**❜**

Ian Wright *on a never-to-happen move to West London*

❝I had a lot of offers but Chelsea were the only club I would have signed for.**❞**

George Best *(sadly the Blues couldn't afford his wage demands)*

❝My ambition is for Chelsea to set the First Division alight inside two seasons. **❞**

Blues boss **Eddie McCeadie**, *May 1977.*
Two seasons later, Chelsea were relegated to the Second Division

❝I feel I am coming to a club where I have a genuine chance of winning something.❞

Clive Wilson *on joining Chelsea in August 1987. Nine months later the Blues were relegated again*

'Seeing this side develop has been like planting a seed and watching it grow like a flower.'

Eddie McCreadie, *February 1977*

❛The Chelsea goal-posts have become my friends, next to all the fellows who have been my team-mates over the years.❜

Peter Bonetti, *April 1976*

❛It will be doomsville for Chelsea. I will stake my reputation on it. They will just collapse.**❜**

Romark, *psychic and hypnotist, on Chelsea's promotion prospects, January 1977*

> ❝Leading Chelsea back to the First Division is the biggest thrill of my life.❞

Ray Wilkins, *May 1977*

❛We always win if Concorde
flies over the Bridge
while we're playing. **❜**

Francis Glibbery, *Chelsea programme
photographer, October 1999*

❝I would like to be in a movie.
I want to be the bad person who
is killed at the end of the movie,
like Gary Oldman in
'Airforce One'. **❞**

Frank Leboeuf, *December 1998*

❝I am bored blue by the company of businessmen. I have absolutely nothing in common with them. I don't like sitting around with a glass in my hand. I don't understand references to Chelsea FC.❞

Conservative politician **Alan Clark**, *1993*

❝ Of all the roles Chelsea are expected to fulfil – highest ticket prices in the league, snazziest restaurant, chairman with the most voluminous beard – winning the title is not one of them. **❞**

Jim White, *writer and Manchester United fan, October 1998*

I was always 'Michael' to my family and friends; I've only been known as 'Micky' since I came to Chelsea, and still don't know how it came about.

Micky Droy, *August 1977*

❝At 35, I'm still looking for improvement in my finishing and heading. Maybe there's still time for me to become a king of finishers! **❞**

Charlie Cooke, *March 1978*

> ❝We remember Peter as one of Chelsea's most skilful, yet modest, players, a model professional and a wonderful club man.❞

Chelsea programme *tribute to Peter Houseman, who died in a car crash, March 1977*

'He was my best mate.
We called each other 'bruv'
and that's what we were like,
brothers. He played up front
with me and I wouldn't
have swapped him for
anyone in the League. '

Peter Osgood, *paying tribute to the late
Ian Hutchinson*

❝Modern-day newspapers would have had a field day just following Chelsea around. We wouldn't have been off the front or back pages.❞

David Webb *on the 70s side, November 2000*

❛I was like Red Adair, saving the team from the drop. But I knew it would only be until the end of the season.**❜**

David Webb *on his brief spell as Blues boss in 1993*

❝Dad supported Arsenal but I was a Chelsea fan. I'll never forget the first game I saw. It was Chelsea at home to West Ham, and I remember Clive Walker was in the side. He was a player who excited me, and I couldn't wait to go back.❞

Paul Merson, *1995*

❝I was a Chelsea fanatic. When my turn to choose the bedroom décor coincided with their FA Cup-winning run of 1970, I gave Mum a Chelsea rosette so she could buy the wallpaper and bed covers in exactly the right colours.❞

Ian Botham, *1994*

❛ Chelsea FC will never lose its identity. Chelsea will be Chelsea for always – and at Stamford Bridge. **❜**

Brian Mears, *Chelsea chairman at a time of financial crisis, April 1977*

It might be poor old Chelsea, or dear old Chelsea, but that's better than no Chelsea at all, isn't it?

Blues boss **Danny Blanchflower**, *February 1979*

' The worst crowd trouble I saw was down at Millwall. In the warm-up, there were people coming out of the crowd with meat-hooks in their heads. I think that's the only time I've been frightened in a game. '

Ian Britton *recalls a terrifying trip to The Den in 1976*

'Last Thursday we received a letter, dated next Monday, complaining about appalling language in the Shed at today's match against Everton. You have been warned!'

Ken Bates, *September 1991*

❝Chelsea went from being a superpower to a dreadful Second Division side more famous for its hooligan element than its team. The whole place became a rancid meat pie crawling with maggots.❞

Alan Hudson, *on the Blues' decline in the late 70s*

❛Quite frankly there are some players here who are simply not good enough.**❜**

Ken Bates, *May 1983*

❝As a shelter for a crowd of football fans, the East Stand is in a class of its own.**❞**

Design *magazine, March 1975*

'We've spent £10 million on the East Stand trying to make a silk purse out of a pig's ear. Everything about that design was appalling. '

Ken Bates, *1999*

❝Kevin Keegan turned to me on the pitch and said, "You've got big problems here." I wasn't going to argue with him. By that time, 1980–81, there were a lot of petty divisions among the players.❞

John Bumstead, *March 2002*

'Even in the warm-up I got booed. 'Chelsea reject!' chants, the lot. All the Leeds players were wetting themselves because they weren't getting any of the stick, it was just me.'

Tony Dorigo *on his return to the Bridge in 1991 with arch-rivals Leeds*

It was obvious from the moment we arrived in Baghdad and saw soldiers carrying machine guns that leisure activities would be limited.

Colin Pates *on Chelsea's trip to Iraq, March 1986*

'I actually don't look forward to Chelsea games these days because they've become real wars.**'**

Tom 'Lofty' Watt, *writer, actor and Arsenal fan*

Keep shooting. Never be afraid to miss.

Kerry Dixon *outlines his goal-scoring philosophy,*
February 1985

❛Somehow it's always a better feeling when you put one in at the Shed end – you get such a roar from those fans.**❜**

Clive Walker, *October 1978*

❝I really wanted to be in a band.**❞**

Pat Nevin *reveals his teenage ambition,*
December 1984

❝I think Pat's dress sense is dreadful. I would like to see him in a nice shirt or proper tie.**❞**

Mary Nevin, *Pat's mother, December 1985*

‟I've always wanted to smack a custard pie in someone's face, just for the devil of it. „

John Sparrow *after fulfilling his dream in January 1978, when a Chelsea-supporting waiter volunteered to be his victim to celebrate Chelsea beating Liverpool 4–2 in the FA Cup*

❝He's the most difficult man to buy a present for. This year, I got him a replica of one of the horse's heads which are featured in the Elgin Marbles in the British Museum.❞

Pam Bates, *then wife of Ken, December 1986*

❛People still come up to me and say thanks for some fantastic memories. That really brings home that you've played a part in this club's great history. It really means something special.**❜**

Kerry Dixon

❝The local TV station asked me how it felt to be joining Southampton. I said, "To be honest, I might be wearing this Southampton shirt, but I still feel like a Chelsea player." As you can imagine, that went down like a lead balloon.❞

Ken Monkou, *on leaving Chelsea in August 1992*

When Vinnie Jones and Mick Harford were in the same side you'd have needed crash helmets to play against them, never mind shin-pads.

Tommy Langley, *June 2002*

❝David broke his leg when only two while playing football, but even that didn't stop him. He was kicking the ball with his leg in plaster, and there were frequent visits to the hospital to get it re-set.❞

Vernon Lee, *father of David, whose Chelsea career was plagued by injury*

❝I never got sent any knickers, but girls would write to ask where I hung out in my spare time and whether I was courting.**❞**

1970s heart-throb **Garry Stanley**

❝I didn't get into girls until I was 18 because of football.**❞**

Roberto Di Matteo

'There's only one real Chelsea kit – the classic kit of the early 70s. The worst has to be the tangerine and grey. What the hell's that got to do with Chelsea?'

Tim Lovejoy, *Soccer AM presenter*

❛Chelsea play in white socks. I always win things in white socks.**❜**

Ruud Gullit, *July 1995*

‘There never was a relationship to begin with between me and Glenn Hoddle, but you could say it deteriorated in that last year. Even the tea lady would have got a game before me! ’

Robert Fleck, *October 2001*

❝There is no club in Britain
I would rather be at. **❞**

Glenn Hoddle, *April 1996, a month before he left*
Chelsea to become England manager

> **❝**I think we were meant to be in a state of continual frustration. I think it might upset everyone more than they know if we actually won something.**❞**

David Baddiel, *September 1995*

❝I'd say the 1997 FA Cup Final was the highlight of my Chelsea career, just because it was such a long time since we'd won a trophy and it meant that people were talking about that team rather than previous Chelsea teams.❞

Steve Clarke, *February 2002*

❝ I really don't mind who we're playing. I'm there home and away every game, and I've always been a little bit surprised by Chelsea fans who seem to be concerned by what the opposition is. **❞**

Matthew Harding, *July 1994*

❝I've been coming to Chelsea for 55 years and it's one of the joys of my life. No matter what concerns I have about work or other matters, for that hour and a half watching out there, it's just magic. I absolutely love it.❞

Lord Attenborough

❝Matthew was always bubbly. He loved being amongst us. That's the way he'd want to be remembered, I reckon. A bubbly, nice, respected Chelsea supporter.❞

Dennis Wise *pays tribute to Matthew Harding, October 1996*

‘Matthew was one of us. In many ways he was like one of the players. There was always a warm heart there for him and from him.’

Ruud Gullit, *October 1996*

"It's good to be back at Wembley. We've been here 12 times. That's more than Chelsea."

Mick Jagger *during The Rolling Stones' 1996 world tour*

❝ One of my most embarrassing confessions is that I'm a Chelsea fan – but the first time I ever went to Stamford Bridge was for a party thrown by Level 42. **❞**

Pop star **Nik Kershaw**, *January 1987*

❝ My first real memory was going to watch Chelsea play Moscow Dynamo. I was eight years old. We crowded through the gate – it was absolutely packed – and I remember being handed over people's heads to get near to the front. **❞**

Comedian **Ted Rogers**, *December 1990*

❛My first-ever commentary game was Liverpool v Chelsea in 1971 at Anfield. A 0–0 draw and a very inconspicuous start to my career. A forgettable match and an even more forgettable commentary.❜

John Motson, *January 1997*

❝I don't buy a player for his entertainment, because then you're going to work in a circus.**❞**

Ruud Gullit, *August 1997*

❝ The best Italian this club has signed is the chef. **❞**

Frank Leboeuf, *January 1999*

❝ If someone needed sorting out, he'd do it. **❞**

Jody Morris *on Dennis Wise, March 2002*

> **❝**Wisey would have made it as a scrum-half. He would have adapted and the game would have knocked that edge out of him.**❞**

England rugby international **Brian Moore**

❝ Dennis Wise could start a fight in an empty room. **❞**

Alex Ferguson, *August 1997*

❮ If Dennis had gone down
I would have served 20 per cent
of his time for him. **❯**

*Football agent **Eric Hall**, after Dennis Wise's*
court case, June 1995

‘Graeme Souness came in raging about a tackle by Dennis Wise on Nigel Clough. In the end I had to tell him, "Calm down, you've just had a triple heart bypass."’

Referee **Keith Hackett**, *November 1994*

❝Wisey said I think too much. But I have to do all his thinking for him.**❞**

Gianfranco Zola, *May 2001*

> ❝My biggest regret is that I never won anything at Stamford Bridge. I loved the club and still do.❞

Clive Walker, *December 1994*

' The fastest man at Stamford Bridge was Clive Walker. I raced him in a 60-metres dash. I won't tell you who won, but we were both dipping for the tape. **'**

Seb Coe, *April 1991*

❛I'm very passionate about antiques because they are like people. You can learn a lot from them.❜

Emmanuel Petit, *March 2002*

> All those bankers earning hundreds of thousands of pounds a year in the City would give it all up for 15 minutes playing for Chelsea.

Former Wycombe boss **Lawrie Sanchez**

❛I think with Chris we now have what we are looking for…**❜**

Gianluca Vialli *hails new signing Chris Sutton, August 1999. In the season that followed Sutton scored just one Premiership goal*

❝Chris Sutton is the 'Waterworld' of strikers – an over-hyped, budget-bursting Kevin Costner-style catastrophe playing at a Premiership theatre near you.❞

The Daily Mirror's **Des Kelly**, *October 1999*

❝They call me the radio because I talk. I love talking. I can't help it. It's a family problem. My wife speaks a lot. My father's always talking. Sometimes at home we need to do a time-out, like in basketball, to stop everybody from talking.❞

Gus Poyet, *May 2000*

In English, the things you use in casinos are chips, but in Italian we call them fish. So I once said, "When the fish are down…" Everybody was, like, "What are you talking about?"

Gianluca Vialli *on his attempts to master the local lingo, June 2002*

> Luca wears some bad, bad underpants – like my grandfather wore. Big white underpants like they used 40 years ago.

Roberto Di Matteo, *December 1996*

❝ Ed de Goey is the worst-dressed man I've ever seen. One pair of jeans, one pair of trainers, one shirt and one haircut. **❞**

John Terry, *December 2002*

❛It was a gamble to come to England but I saw what Ole Gunnar Solskjaer achieved and I thought, "I can do better than that." ❜

Tore Andre Flo, *September 1997*

Have you seen the size of Jimmy Floyd Hasselbaink's hooter? It's the biggest in the club. But cop a look at John Terry's, because that's not far behind. It's a beaut.

Jody Morris, *May 2001*

Brutissimi! Terrible! It was one of the worst games of my life!

*Manchester United goalkeeper **Massimo Taibi** recalls the Blues' 5–0 win in October 1999*

❛Q: What time is it?

A: Five past United!**❜**

Ken Bates *cracks a joke after the same game*

❛I believe the last man to score five times in a Chelsea shirt was David Mellor.❜

Tony Banks MP, *July 1997*

‘I've asked John Major if he's going to start coming again. He gets a bloody good pension as a former prime minister, so he might even be able to afford a season ticket.’

Tony Banks MP, *July 1997*

'Luca thinks he looks like Bruce Willis, but I think he looks more like Bruce Forsyth.'

Aaron Lincoln, *Chelsea kit man, May 1999*

❝I wouldn't change one of my players for one of the Manchester United players.**❞**

Gianluca Vialli, *October 1999*

'Villa were like some two-bob team trying to get through on penalties.'

Ken Bates *on the 2000 FA Cup Final, which Chelsea won 1–0*

❛I think Luca dropped it, and then tried to blame it on me! I'm not quite sure who dropped it, actually. It wasn't me, honest!**❜**

Dennis Wise *explains a dent in the lid of the FA Cup, November 2000*

❝When Ruud made it clear that he wanted a package that would cost us £3.7m plus bonuses we knew it was the end of the road.❞

Ken Bates *on the sacking of Ruud Gullit, February 1998*

❝We had to make a change.
There is no easy way to do it.
Do you go for a shot in
the head, or a death from
a thousand cuts?❞

Ken Bates *on the sacking of Gianluca Vialli,*
September 2000

"I can look back and say, "I've lived," and that's all down to this old funny game."

Gianluca Vialli, *February 2000*

‘When I got sacked by Chelsea, I didn't realise how much it would hurt.’

John Hollins, *November 1997, nine years after Ken Bates gave him his P45*

> **'** I think Mr Ranieri will kick a few backsides, but only in a most pleasant manner. **'**

Ray Wilkins, *September 2000*

❝You may not have heard of me before I came to you last month, but I had heard of you.**❞**

Claudio Ranieri's *message to Chelsea fans,*
October 2000

❝Chelsea are being managed by Frank Spencer, the well-intentioned but accident-prone half-wit from 'Some Mothers Do 'Ave Em'.**❞**

The Sun's **Steven Howard** *is unimpressed by Claudio Ranieri, November 2001*

❝ I feel very akin to the English warrior spirit – the spirit of fighting for every ball. **❞**

Claudio Ranieri, *May 2001*

❝You should never go back in life. You don't see many people out with their ex-wives, do you?**❞**

Ken Bates, *ruling out a Bridge return for Dennis Wise, September 2002*

❝I've heard Batesy's a pearler because he kicks every ball. Poor Suzannah must have loads of bruises.**❞**

Dennis Wise, *February 1998*

❝Every time I see him it reminds me to buy a pint of milk on the way home.**❞**

*Chelsea kitman **Aaron Lincoln** on Mikael Forssell's pale features*

❝With Hasselbaink currently bubbling like a pot of molten lava, it's going to take a defence clothed in asbestos to avoid further incineration.❞

Hot stuff from The Sun's **Steven Howard**, *January 2002*

❛I wanted to build an exciting new Chelsea, providing such entertainment that the players got a standing ovation from the fans even if they lost.**❜**

Ken Bates *outlines his football vision, May 1984*

‘In the 70s, it was Leeds; in the 80s it was Liverpool; and, in the 90s, it has been Manchester United. Now Chelsea are the team for the millennium. The team that everybody loves to hate, that is.’

The Observer's **Ian Ridley**, September 1998

‘Graeme Le Saux takes a lot of stick from people because he's wise, but it's just the way he is and he's a great geezer.’

Frank Lampard, *December 2002*

❛Yoghurts are down at Asda.**❜**

Graeme Le Saux, *when asked for his 'Save of the Month', September 1998*

❝Quite simply, the little man is a genius.**❞**

Dennis Wise *on Gianfranco Zola*

> In 'Something About Mary', there's a fella called Ted. He's a pure lookalike for Franco Zola.

Jody Morris

❝I used to share a room with Gianfranco Zola but I had to throw him out because he snored so much.**❞**

Roberto Di Matteo, *February 1999*

"If I was having a race with my mum and I was expected to beat her by 50 yards, I'd like to beat her by 60 yards. I love winning."

Frank Sinclair, *December 1996*

'The day I walked through the door I just thought what a magnificent ground, magnificent stadium, fantastic name, and a tremendous location. Why isn't this club bigger than Arsenal and Spurs? '

Ken Bates, *July 1997*

❛When my team looked into clubs with the best possible fundamentals and prospects, Chelsea really did come first. The ground, the location, the Champions League qualification, the staff and players and fan support were, and remain, a wonderful foundation.❜

Roman Abramovich, *August 2003*

❝I was a complete unknown when I came here and Chelsea were a complete unknown in France, so it's been a fantastic love affair.**❞**

Frank Leboeuf, *February 2001*

❝I want to stay here because I love the city, I love the club and I love the supporters.**❞**

Carlo Cudicini, *May 2002*

❝There were eggs and sausages for the staff on the plane, but just cereals and toast for the players. All the lads were pointing at me, saying, "No hot food, he's the striker!"❞

*Club masseur **Billy McCulloch** is the victim of a players' prank on a European trip, October 2002*

❝I want to play against Carlton. He's saying to me his street is the main street, so I said, "What do you want, an away game or a home game?"**❞**

Mario Melchiot *challenges Carlton Cole and friends to a 'jumpers for goal-posts' match, October 2002*

"It was laughable, no? I mean, how can the captain of Chelsea, in the middle of the season, leave the club? To go to Manchester? I mean, it's not possible..."

Marcel Desailly, *on a rumoured move to Manchester United, April 2002*

❝Marcel Desailly is an inspiration – the best-loved, most-valued member of the team. Everyone calls him The Commandant.**❞**

Adrian Mutu, *October 2003*

❝You don't get many one-club players nowadays, but I definitely want to stay at Chelsea for the rest of my career.**❞**

John Terry, *November 2001*

❝I think John Terry's got a hell of a future. The only difference between him and me is that, when I tackled, they didn't get up. ❞

Ron Harris, *May 2001*

❝If one day I reach international level, I would like to play for France. Why? Simply because I like the way they play.**❞**

Graeme Le Saux, *March 1990*

"I played for Napoli and it was blue. I play for Chelsea and it's blue. Italy is blue. Blue belongs to me, my life."

Gianfranco Zola, *January 2002*

❝When I was at school,
I preferred football to cricket.
Until cricket took over, I'd play
football on Saturday mornings
and then go to watch Chelsea
in the afternoons, standing in
the Shed.**❞**

Alec Stewart, *September 1990*

❛I don't like to lump Chelsea in with all the other London clubs. They are too individualistic for that. Middlesex has been Chelsea's county since AD703 and that's how I like to think of them, a Middlesex club. ❜

Astrologer **Russell Grant**, *September 1990*

❝ He might be a billionaire but he is already regarded as one of us – a Chelsea, or Chelski, Boy. **❞**

Ken Bates *on Roman Abramovich, August 2003*

❛I don't want to change what works. I just want to help take what we have at Stamford Bridge to the next level. And I want us all to work hard and have a lot of fun doing it.**❜**

Roman Abramovich, *August 2003*

❝A brave man dies once, a coward dies a million times.**❞**

Ken Bates, *at the time of Chelsea's controversial trip to Israel to play Hapoel Tel Aviv in October 2001*

❝I don't seek publicity, it seeks me.**❞**

Ken Bates

❝When you play every three days, the victory is a good vitamin.**❞**

Claudio Ranieri, *January 2002, during a busy schedule of fixtures*

❝I really envy Ruud because he was so cool and calm. The way I am doing this job is a little bit different. I can't get away from thinking about football 24 hours a day.**❞**

Gianluca Vialli, *February 1998*

❝ Everybody is talking about Chelsea. Real Madrid is no different to anyone. There's lots of interest. Everybody is talking about the ambition of the London club, Chelsea. **❞**

Claude Makelele, *September 2003*

❝I had one agent phoning up saying, "I have the honour of representing one of the world's greatest players, he needs no introduction." I said, "You're right, I don't want to meet him."❞

Ken Bates *keeps his cheque-book shut, summer 2002*

'When I signed for Chelsea, all the papers made out I was an alcoholic and here for the nights out and the booze. But I'm just here to play football.'

Damien Duff, *October 2003*

❝I could see little similarities, but obviously it was so over the top. The captain's out all day drinking and you're thinking, "This is what people are going to think we're really like."❞

Frank Lampard, *on the hit TV show, 'Footballers Wives'*

❝Germans don't play rugby at all, but I like it. I like the impacts!**❞**

Robert Huth, *September 2003*

❛You cannot describe the feeling of scoring a goal. No one will understand unless they have done it themselves. **❜**

Eidur Gudjohnsen, *January 2002*

"You alwight mate, innit, innit? Speaking cockney is so funny especially when you first come over. The first time you hear it you think, "What is that?""

Mario Melchiot, *October 2002*

❝I would be happiest, when I'm 50 or so, for people to say, "I remember you – you were a good player."**❞**

Graeme Le Saux, *January 1990*

❝Sometimes it is good to score after 43 seconds… and sometimes it is good to last a little longer.❞

Roberto Di Matteo

❝The appointment of Jose Mourinho is all about building on the foundations which we have already established at Chelsea. His record of sustained success makes him perfect for what we want to achieve.**❞**

Chelsea chief executive **Peter Kenyon**,
June 2004

'Please don't call me arrogant, but I'm a European champion and I think I'm a special one.'

Jose Mourinho *on his arrival at Chelsea, June 2004*

I I was not happy about these stories about me wanting an English passport and Sven's job. It was all ridiculous. **J**

Jose Mourinho *rules himself out of contention to be the next England manager, October 2005*

The Chelsea Mourinho is the same guy as the Porto Mourinho. You have to prove youself in every training session, to demand more of yourself the whole time.

Paulo Ferreira, *who played under Mourinho at Porto before joining Chelsea, October 2005*

On paper we've got the best squad around, best manager and we're hungrier than anyone else. Put those three together and you'll never be far off.

Damien Duff *anticipates more success, September 2005*

❛One of my ambitions when I finish playing football is to get a pilot's licence. I've already started practising on computer simulations with a friend and researching it on the internet.**❜**

*The sky's the limit for **Carlo Cudicini**,*
August 2005

❝My hair is difficult, it's a problem! It doesn't always look healthy. But there's nothing I can do about it. If it was up to me, I would have chosen a different kind of hair.❞

Every day's a bad hair day for **Ricardo Carvalho**,
January 2005

"Without our fantastic supporters, there would not be a Chelsea Football Club and we will never forget that. In the future, we hope to bring you more joy than you have experienced in the last hundred years."

Roman Abramovich, *summer 2005*

'Roman Abramovich is turning Chelsea into one of Europe's elite clubs, and I think it's a great thing. The fans are getting to see great players and that's what it's all about. '

Soccer AM *presenter and Chelsea fan*
Tim Lovejoy, *December 2004*

❝I've been here since I was 14 and to be made captain of such a great team is a dream come true.**❞**

John Terry, *September 2004*

❝I think he's a fantastic captain because he's Chelsea through and through. He plays like he's got feelings for the club.❞

*Former skipper **Ron 'Chopper' Harris** on John Terry, October 2004*

❛All of my players were magnificent and deserved to win, no doubt. We now have the first title and almost for sure we will have the second one. And that will be the big one.**❜**

Jose Mourinho *looks forward to more success after Chelsea's Carling Cup triumph, February 2005*

❝I think he is one of those people who is a voyeur. He likes to watch other people. There are some guys who, when they are at home, have a big telescope to see what happens in other families. He speaks, speaks, speaks about Chelsea.❞

Jose Mourinho *has a pop at Arsene Wenger, October 2005*

❝Andrew Flintoff. He's the man of the moment. He's just a normal, good lad and the best cricketer in the world. And I chose him because he got absolutely rat-arsed on the parade!❞

Frank Lampard *nominates his favourite non-footballing sportsman, September 2005*

❝ I want to give a personal thank you to my team-mates, every single one of you. I love you all. **❞**

An emotional **John Terry** *after Chelsea won the Premiership, April 2005*

'The day at Bolton when we won the League will always be special, but to get my hands on the trophy at Charlton and lift it, it was the best thing in my life so far.

John Terry *reflects on Chelsea's Premiership title triumph, September 2005*

> By 2014 we want to be internationally recognised as the No. 1 club. It's a very ballsy vision but one that has captured the interest of the owner.

Peter Kenyon *reveals the extent of Chelsea's ambition, November 2006*

❝ I am manager today, I am the manager until the end of the season and I believe I will be the manager until the end of 2010. If I believe what I read in the press there are 11 candidates for my job but I don't get influenced by that. **❞**

Mourinho *responds to questions about his future at Stamford Bridge, January 2007*

❝Jose is the best in the business, there's no doubt about that, and I am sure he will be for the next 20 years. That's what we want at Chelsea, the best and only the best.**❞**

*Skipper **John Terry** wants Mourinho to stay at the Bridge*

> **❝**I would be disappointed if he was leaving. I have enjoyed his company in the times we meet after the game and things like that. He has a good personality and I enjoy the competition against him.**❞**

And so, surprisingly, does **Sir Alex Ferguson**

❝ I know full well that I'm not a greedy person. I've not come here for money. I've come here because I want to win things and I have a good chance of winning things at Chelsea. **❞**

Ashley Cole *signs from Arsenal, September 2006*

❝People will always say the best player at Chelsea has been Gianfranco Zola but I would say Peter was the greatest. He was such a strong player, a big fellow who scored goals and scared defenders.**❞**

Ron 'Chopper' Harris *pays tribute to the late Peter Osgood, March 2006*

" We are like soldiers going out to perform our duty. It is a big battle ahead and we have to conquer the enemy to move forward and succeed. "

Michael Essien *declares war on title rivals Manchester United, November 2006*

> **I** hope the club can help me fulfil my ambition to become one of the top players in the world. I really wanted to be a Chelsea player. Finally, I got it right. **"**

John Obi Mikel *joins Chelsea after a protracted transfer saga, August 2006*

❝ I know I am not risking my life by playing again, and that is the main thing. **❞**

Brave **Petr Cech**, *returns to action in January 2007, three months after a horrific head injury at Reading*

❝If he's not the best striker in Europe, I don't know where there's a better one. His all-round game is fantastic. He's scoring spectacular goals. That's Didi and it's great to have a striker playing like that.**❞**

An excited **Frank Lampard** *acknowledges Didier Drogba's scintillating form, October 2006*

❝The fans are awesome, every player wants to play in a place where he is fully accepted and I've found that here at Chelsea.❞

A contented **Drogba***, November 2006*

'Chelsea deserve all the plaudits they will get and, especially on their home form, they are worthy champions.'

Sir Alex Ferguson *concedes Chelsea are worthy winners of a second successive title, April 2006*

❝It's a massive achievement. United have dominated this league for a while, but now we're putting down our marker and proving that we're capable of doing that.**❞**

Joe Cole *relishes Chelsea's success*

❝I am as convinced as I was three or four months ago we are going to win the title.**❞**

Mourinho *in typically confident mood, December 2006*

❝My bad qualities are that I don't care about my image and because of that I don't care about the consequences of what I say and the consequences of what I do.❞

Mourinho, *candid as ever, December 2006*

'Stand up for the special one.'

Chelsea fans *chant in appreciation of Jose Mourinho*